summer rugby

"In my Life,
Rugby is not a sport,
is not a work, is not a
game, It's a Belief
!!!!"

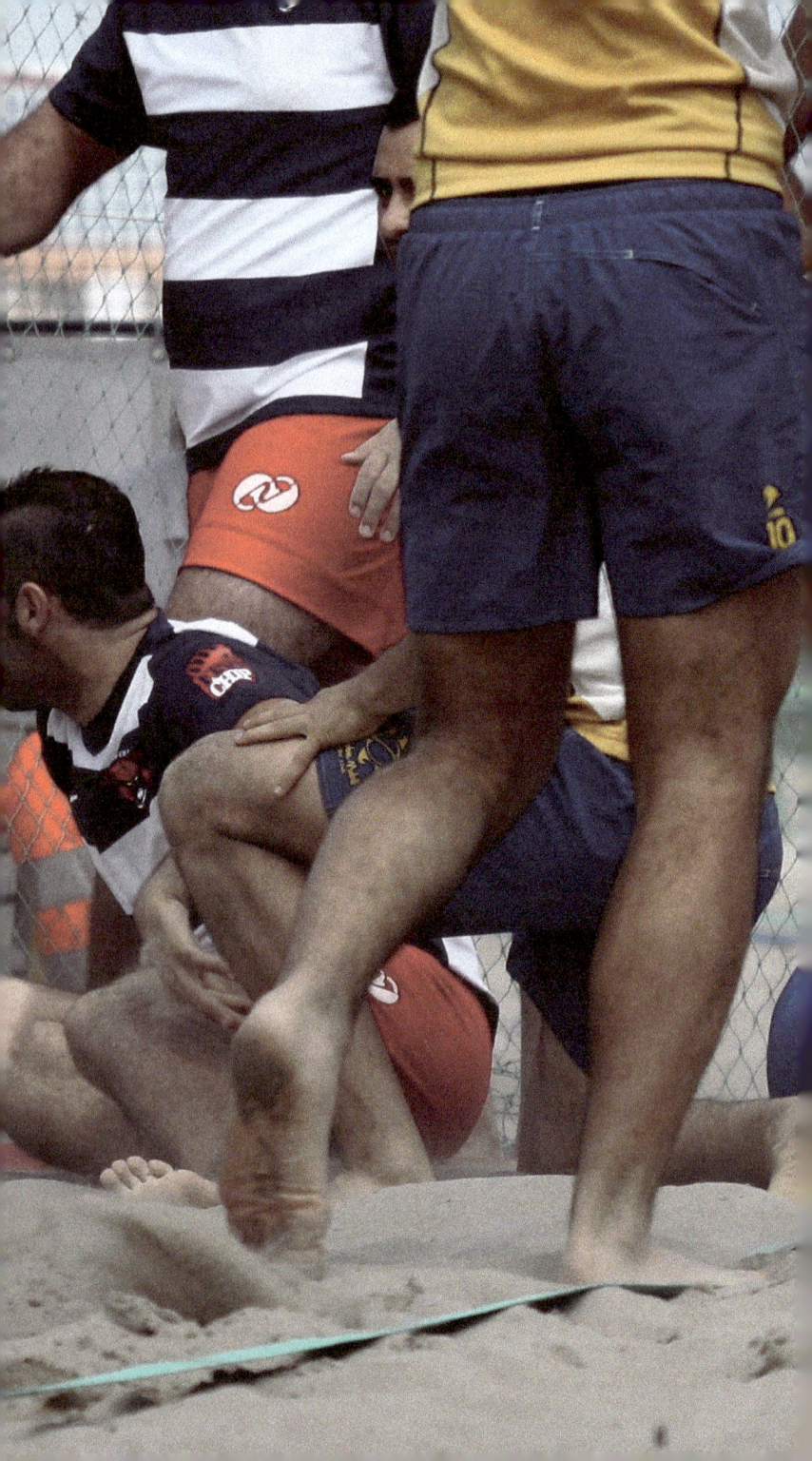

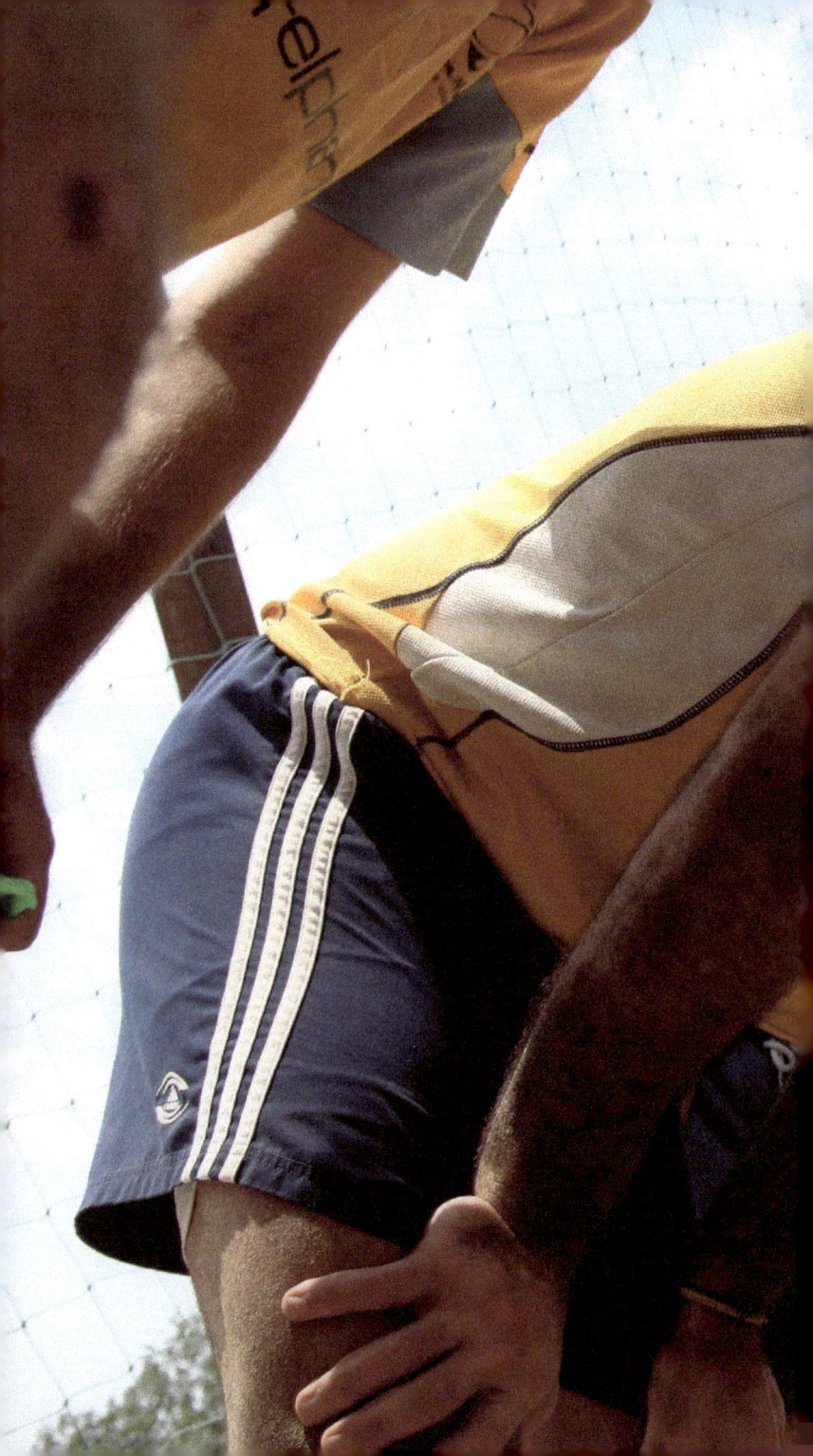

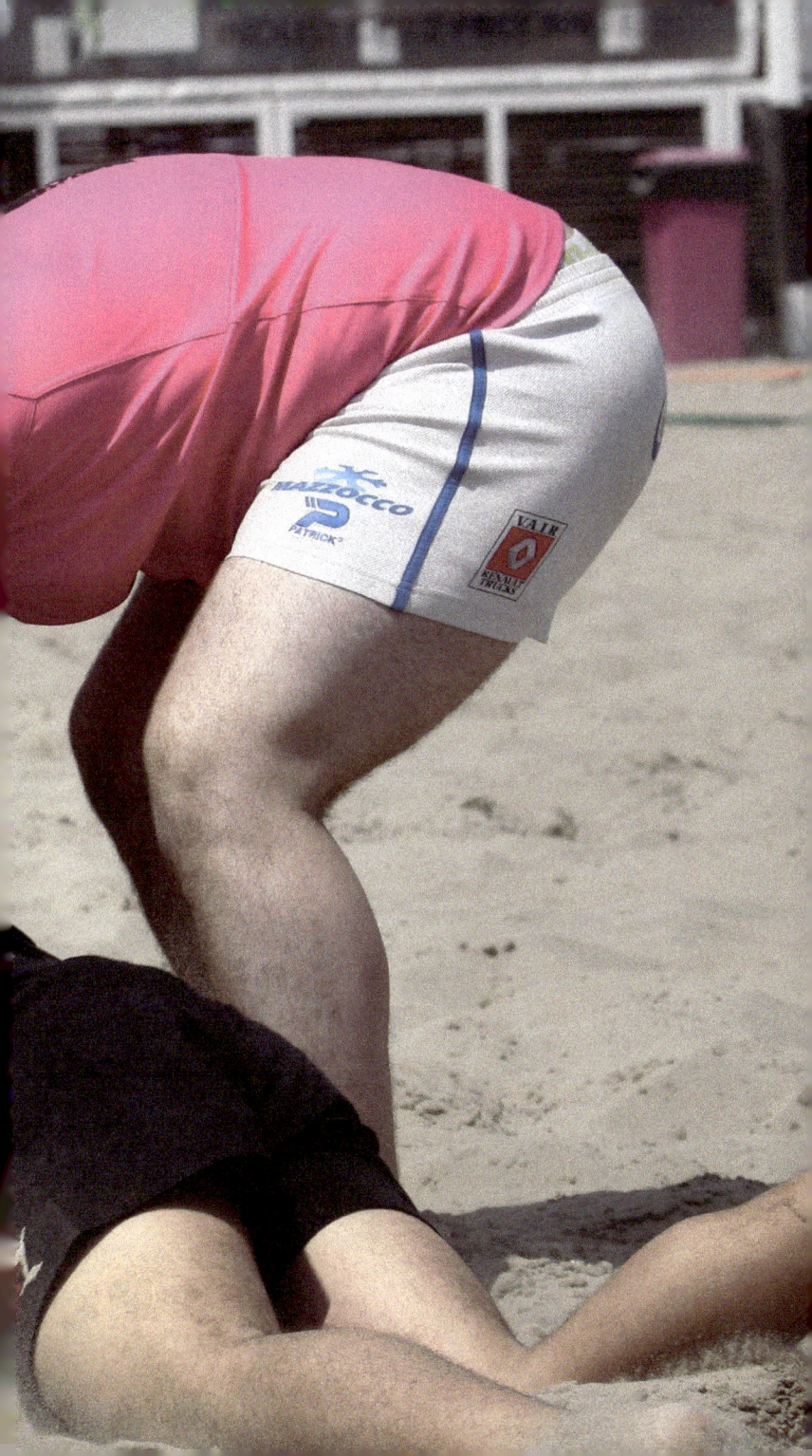

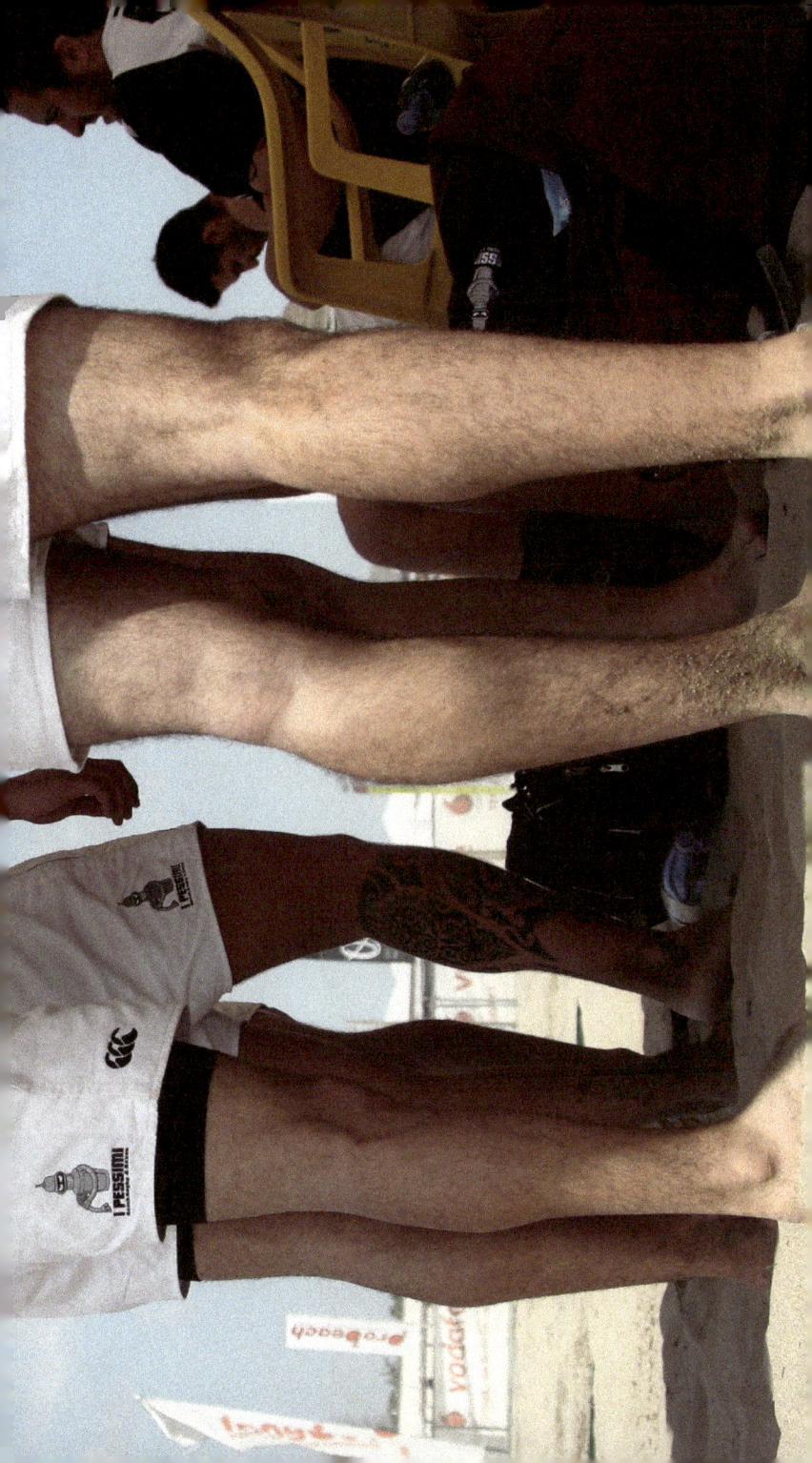

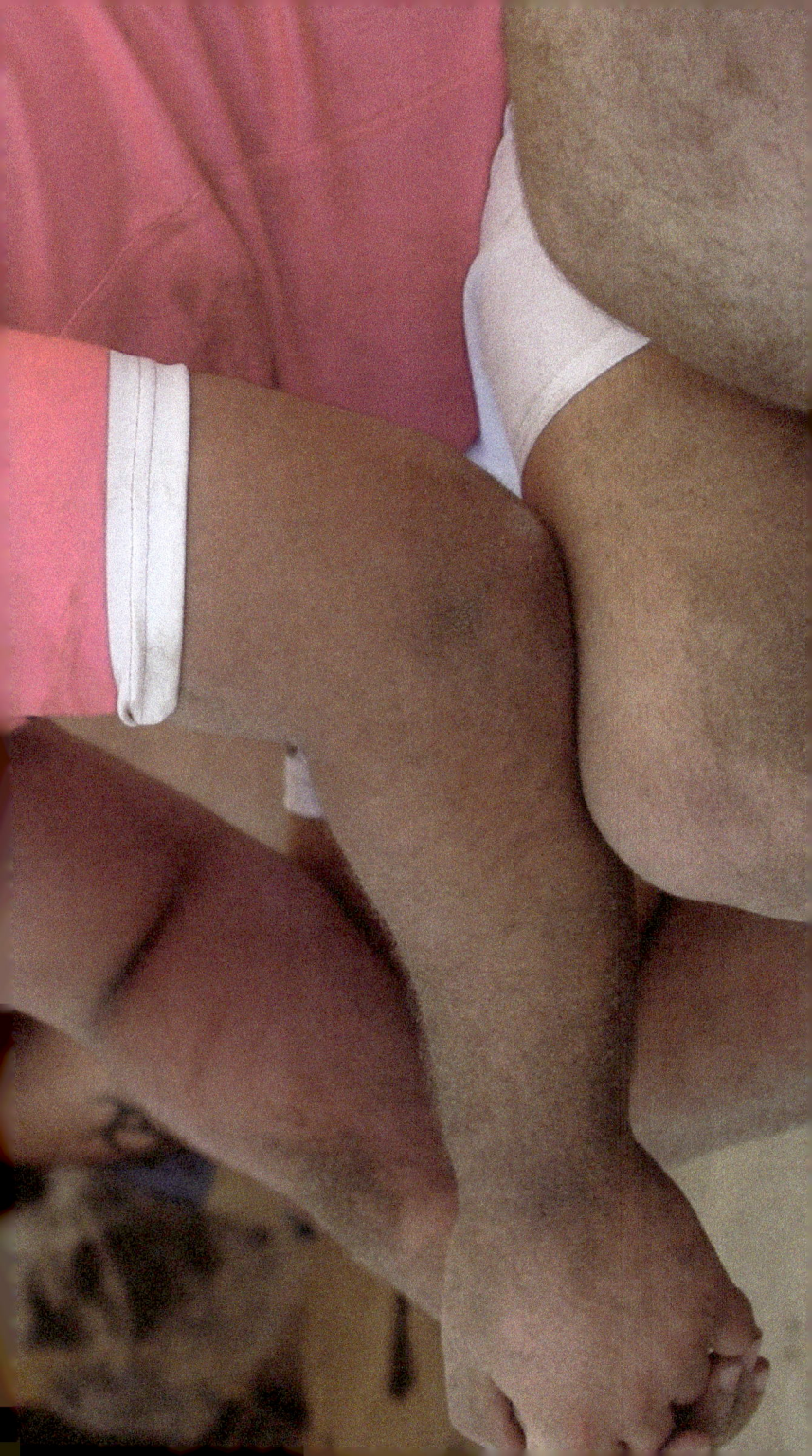

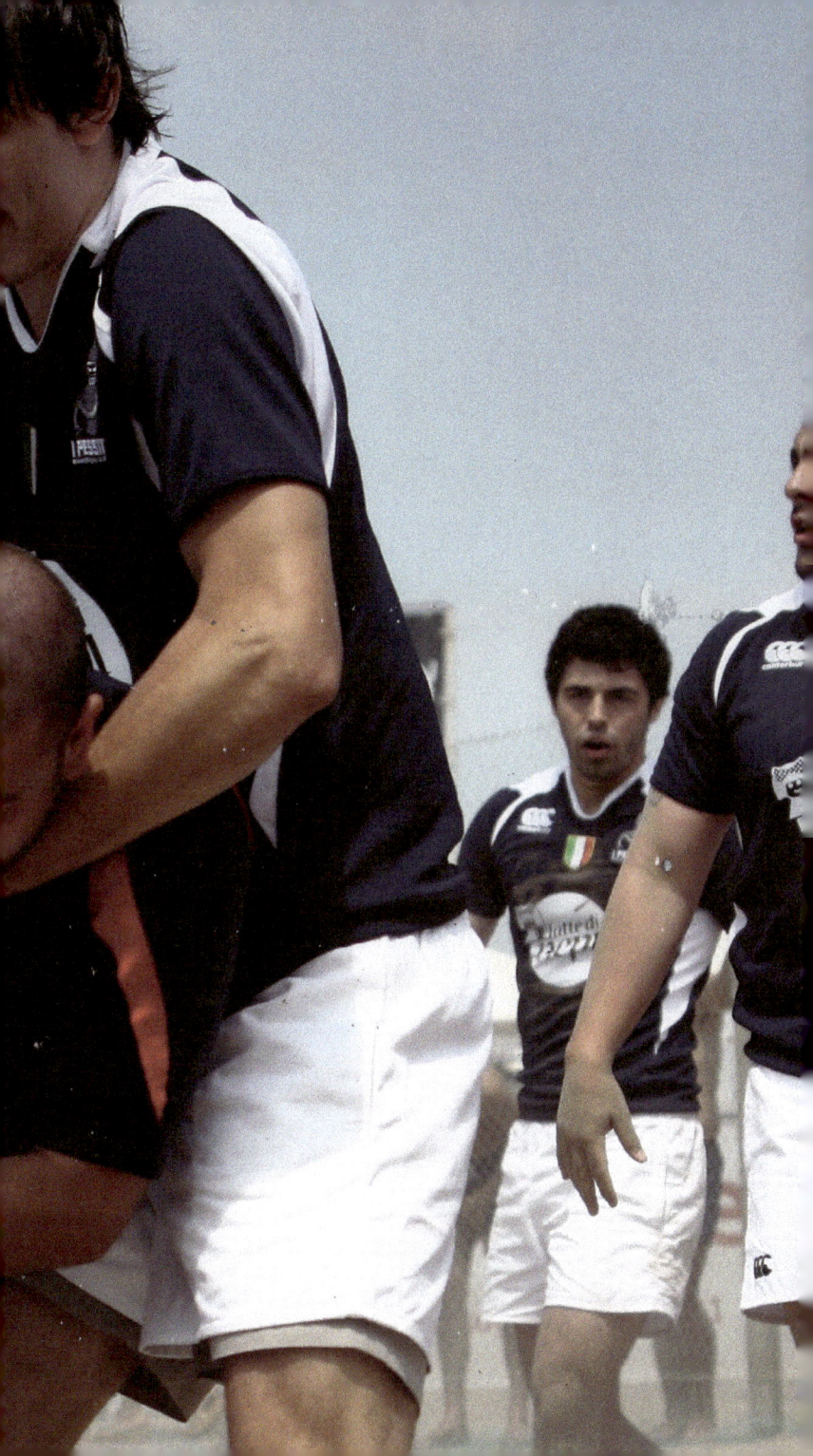

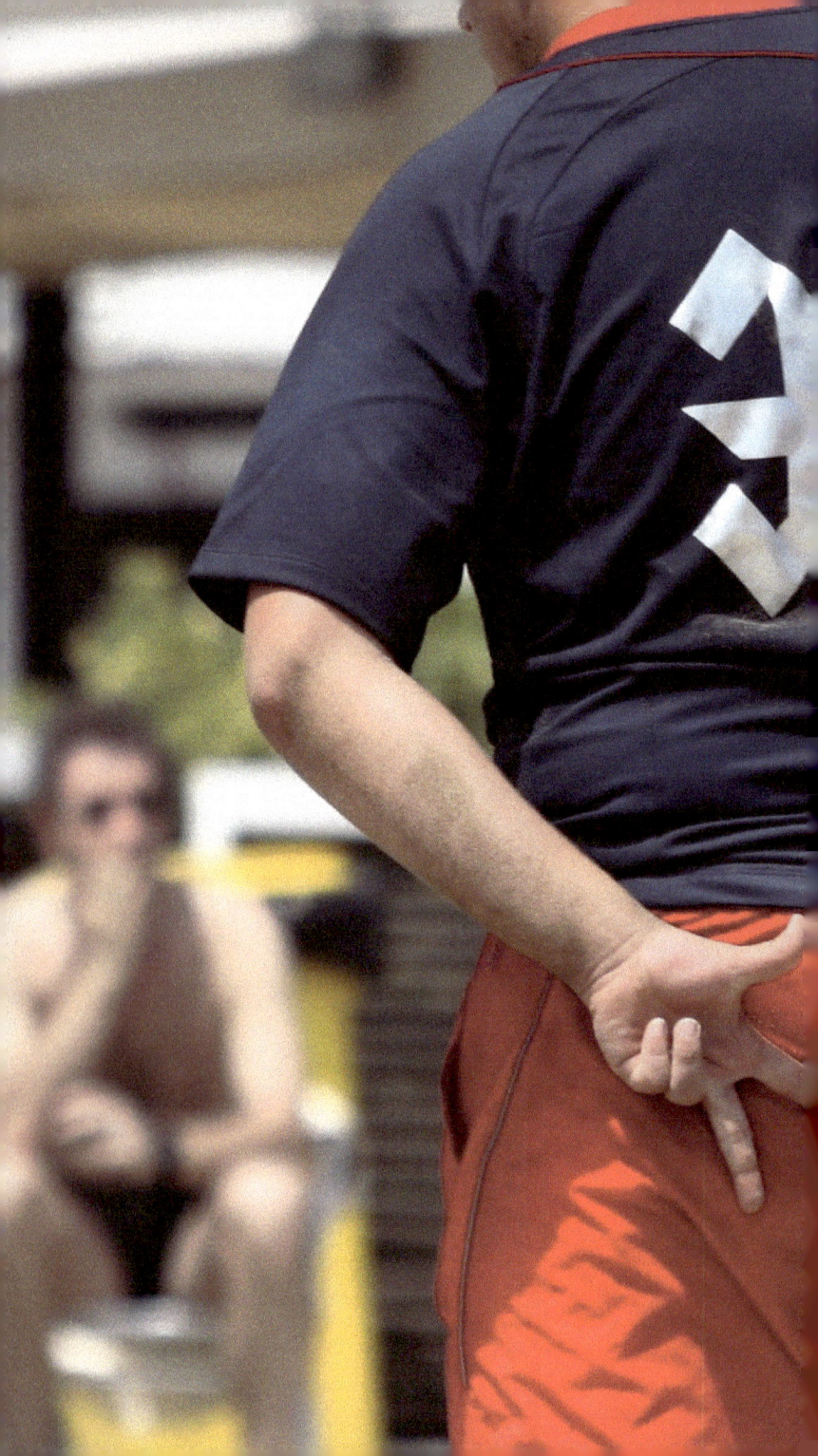

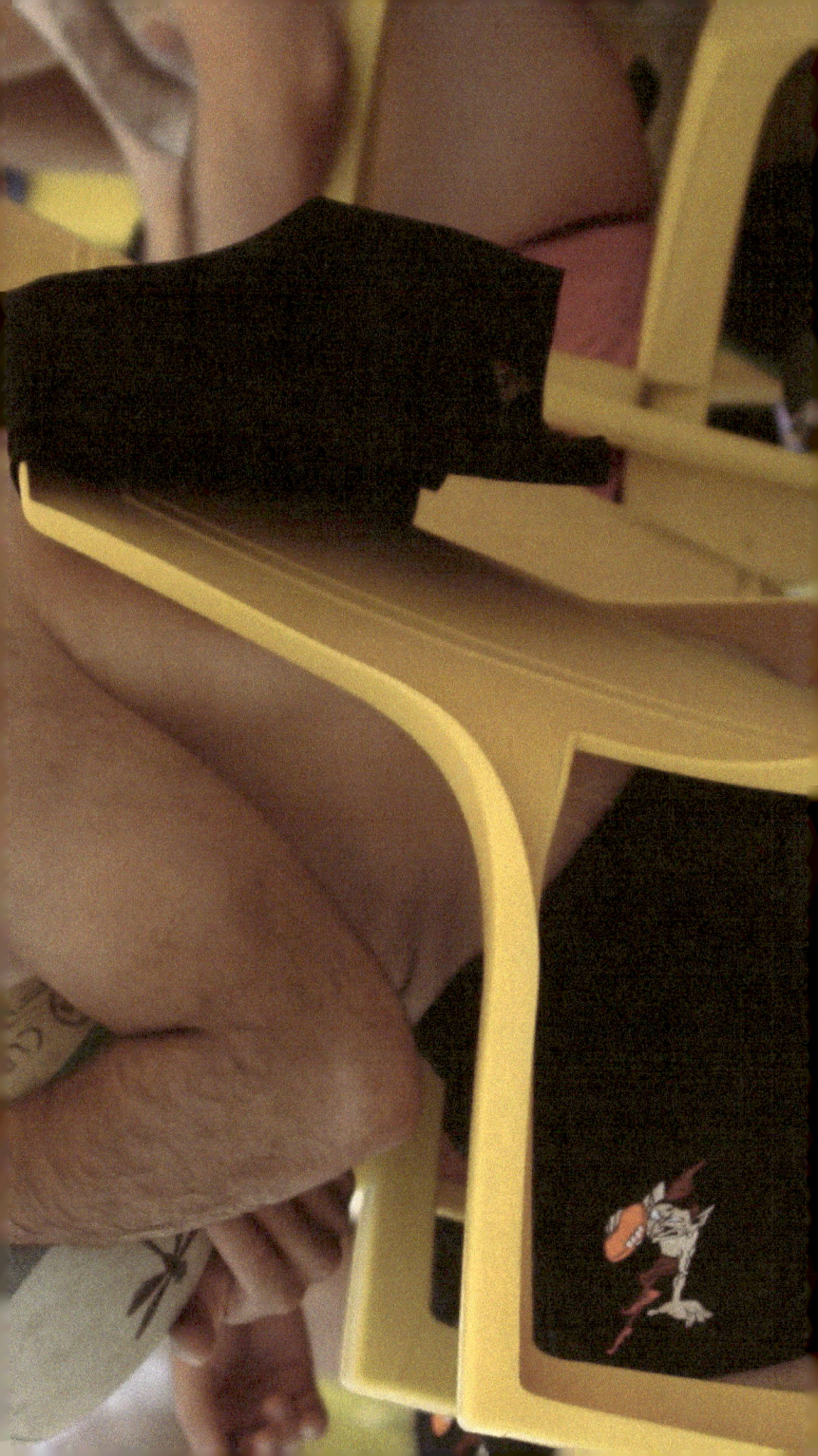

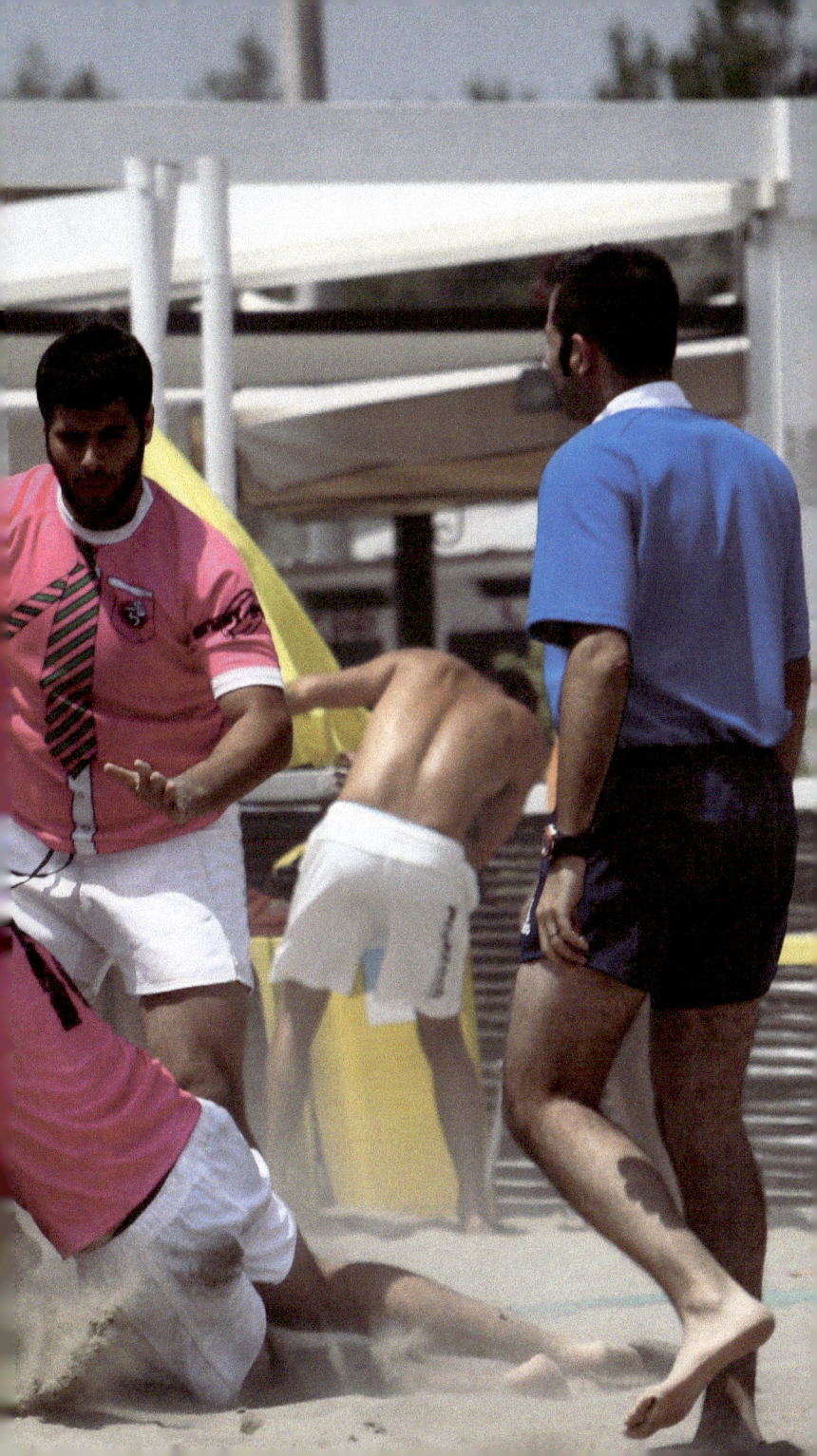

CPSIA information can be obtained
at www.ICGtesting.com
Printed in the USA
BVHW021437100719
553079BV00011B/75/P

9 780464 024774